Feed and Disc

Feed and Discern

SOME WORDS OF WISDOM, SOME POEMS, SOME LIFE LESSONS

sheila atienza

Privilege Digital Media

Feed and Discern: Some Words of Wisdom, Some Poems, Some Life Lessons

Hardcover ISBN-13:
978-1-990408-22-9

Paperback ISBN-13:
978-1-990408-07-6

E-book ISBN:
978-1-990408-08-3

SUBJECTS:

POETRY / Subjects & Themes / Inspirational & Religious

BODY, MIND & SPIRIT / Inspiration & Personal Growth

SELF-HELP / Motivational & Inspirational

THEMA SUBJECTS:

Christian life & practice
Mind, body, spirit: thought & practice
Assertiveness, motivation & self-esteem

Contents

to you
who seek wisdom

1

outward

in looking outward
what do we see
a day that can spark
through a number of hours
until
our spirit in
anxiety
goes
through the two in-between
nights of darkness

yet again
the spirit would disentangle
we shall
witness
another unclouded
shimmering day

we see a bright, pleasant atmosphere
we immerse
through it, for a while
it takes us into a web
of promises
putting one's head in the clouds

then the day breaks
and our spirits
are onto another round
of affliction
as though we shut
our senses
seeing no other path
but to remain
in anguish

why must this
happen
why must this
go on, again and again
the spirit in torment
was asking
yet again

how are we to thrive
in this earthly life
should one pass through
a test of
enduring pain

i can't seem to comprehend
but within me, i know, that in essence
we look outward
to allow another bright day
to begin

how well
have you looked
from within
the question
that we should be asking

and if we are
to look through
the hours
we have in our
hands, we could be wiser
and see what finally brings us
awareness
to be in touch deep within us

for in reality
we hope, we dream, we aim
until we see
outward
to see light
once again

* * *

2

in between the waiting

you put yourself out there
yet no one notices you
you wonder
should you keep it there
longer

you waited long hours
of many days
you said to yourself
you would like to keep waiting
and waiting
year after year

fast forward to where
you are
now, still
no one bothers

"what should i do?"
you ask yourself this time
and many more times
yet you seem to find
not even a single answer

truth is
in this world, you are not alone
a million more others
ask the same question
and one, two, or even more
would come to some point
of realization

yes, it is not easy
to go out of
one's comfort
zone
one may cry out for help
get tired and exhibit
a moan of desperation
and may put oneself
in isolation

you are caught up in
a moment when you are in
the verge of giving up

but then if you decide
to finally give up
you could end up
asking another question

what if
one day comes
the odds turn in your favour
how would you
then respond

of course the rarity
of the circumstance is apparent
like getting in luck with
some lottery or other
sorts of games

in between the waiting
why not tap into your
inner being
listen to your inner voice
who knows
what it could actually
be telling

looking into the bigger picture
why not zone in
to a
smaller horizon

in between the waiting
you might as well find
little joys
in whatever it is
you are doing

* * *

3

state of emptiness

an empty stomach
waits for some kind of food to fill it up
until it is satisfied
it can rest
it can relax

an empty mind
waits for some kind of food to fill it up
some inspiration or boost
some words of wisdom
until it can realize
that things are happening in its course

it is with such a state of emptiness
that we find ourselves
seeking for what matters
in each or every part of our senses
it signals an opportunity
to find what it means with our reality
until it reaches
its fulfillment

so don't fear
leave anxiety behind
even if you are scared
even if you may be absorbed
with the thought of nothingness
or despair

very soon, you will find
this once dull, hollow
state of emptiness
will then be gone

you can then
laugh
you can then
have fun

* * *

4

~

blanket

love or indebtedness
such mighty words
that could help one
get through the entirety
of one's existence
if not, part of the chosen
journey

love or indebtedness
such powerful words
like a blanket
that could cover
partly or entirely
a body
that might have been
wounded
or that might have been
struck
by a knife or an
object
sharp as it might seem
there persist something
that could be
troubling

when will the degree
or amount of pain ever
find its way
to reach its
finality
or
will its shadow
haunt us forever

does a person always
have to look back and say
to oneself and
someone else
"forever
grateful i shall be," or even apt to say
"forever, i am indebted."

going forward
we must know
deep within the heart
love can only reach
perfection
if we say we are ready
to take
what we ought to do
on this earth

* * *

5

hail

flowers and kiss
some women may wish
true enough
that could make
one feel in bliss

a simple way
to sum up
how to put one
in comfort and
ease

you see
one
can't help but wonder
such gestures
may seem easy

but why does it
take so much effort
to greet one
lovingly and
peacefully

hail to you and others
start your day
with hope and
cheer

you see
a simple greet
could boost one's
spirit

one can keep
going
and one
could feel great

hail to you and others
the day is shining
you look dazzling
keep your aura glowing

* * *

6

all along

all along, you were
building a great armour
a shield that can protect you from
harm

you just don't see that
as you may be busy
looking at
other aspects of your life

all along, you were glowing
you just don't appreciate that
as you have been through
some bumps and mistakes
through the rides
that you take

all along, you are making
the best of what you can
be
you just don't see that
as you may have gone
through some of the ups and
downs
and even
through the lowest point in
your life

all along, you
are becoming
the person you
ought to be
you just don't see
that
as you may be
consumed with your present
circumstances

all along, you are
a confident being
you just don't realize that
as you may be
accustomed
to your
old self

what you must
recognize though
in the process
all those things
that you have been through
those are
the little steps
that you had
to go through
to be where you are

along the way
those little steps
will take you to
where you
ought to go
to where you
should be

* * *

7

sight

do not lose sight of a city
for one structure
or building
for in life
we may capture
charm, alluring view
that may not be obvious
but of value

in truth
we may be stunned by
one thing
but lose sight
of the beauty
of the whole
surrounding

we tend to work or
be busy with
something
but we lose
balance, and
even miss out on a lot of things

we lose
control
of our time, resources
and
even our ability to
discern

sometimes
we may need to call on
ourselves
to redirect
our focus and
energy

* * *

8

reimagining

we may carry out
a simple task
yet sometimes
we can't help
but feel restless

and therefore end up
seeing
life
in an angle
that is too complex

when we try to
reimagine
the bigger scenario
we build up hope
we look through a new
outlook and view

even if we
lose track of our direction
we could always try
to revisit
our vision

we could regain
our strength
we could find
our motivation
and a reason
to keep moving, to keep reaching
for our goal

when we allow the countless
stars to align
when we allow ourselves to wait
for the appropriate
time
and as we enrich our faith
as we persist
as we believe
perhaps, then
we can finally find
the path
to our destination
even we can call it
our fate

* * *

9

~

route

as we go on
to our adventure
several options
we find
the route
that could take us
through
the better
direction

we seek to find
a way to
take us
fast
and we hope to
take steps
without, if not lesser, mishaps

but as one could tell
we could always
end up
deep
in the well
if not trapped

hardly
we could move up
and see light
that could guide our journey
throughout

worse
who knows
until when
we could be stuck
in an unforeseen stop

* * *

10

what you say

you say life is
hard
but you managed
to survive

you say life is
peculiar
but you managed
to get rid of your fears

you say life
can be puzzling
but you managed to
find its meaning

you say life is
a mysterious event
in which human beings
can participate

you say you have been
in your
life's
darkest hour

but you managed
to see
through the day's
finest hour

you see sunrise
and even see more
there, you are in awe
and wait
for what it
promises

you have a choice
to keep going
listen to your unique voice
or witness a new beginning

until the day is over
you have a chance to play
know when to follow rules
or when to break away

life is
just like that
you can be onto
some thrill
experience some chills
but you can always
climb the hill
be in life's
some kind of spectacle

at the end of the day
who knows
you can win some battles
and then some more
go through a cycle
that can lead you back
to a life
that you have long wanted
for yourself

* * *

11

a never-ending why

why do we expect a lot
when we cannot
be sure
if we will get it or not

why does it take
a lot of guts
to do things
you could be good at

why does it seem quite an effort
to express words of thanks
for such things that you requested
you received, you consumed

why does it seem so hard sometimes
to listen and
focus our mind
on things worthy of our attention

why does it seem so hard and heavy
to say sorry
when you could feel guilty
for not expressing it

why does it seem
difficult to learn to
trust again after someone
has offended you

why do we complain a lot
when we are not
willing to do
some effort to work things out

why does it seem awkward, sometimes, or
odd to just express your
appreciation and fondness
on things you
like and enjoy

why do we strive
for perfection
when we know
it is so hard to attain

why does it seem
so hard
to face reality
while pretending is not

why does it seem so hard
to express
your regard of yourself
when it should be the easiest

* * *

12

~

some time, a chance

give yourself some time
you
may
go through some
denial

give yourself some time
acceptance
does
not
happen in a flash

give yourself some time
channel
your emotion
and at some point
you would come out better of your shell

give yourself a chance
to understand and see
going through such
an emotional state is
only temporary

give yourself an assurance
whatever
you may experience
today
you will learn to overcome

give yourself a chance
to see
life
in its most exquisite
form

give yourself a chance
to start
believing in yourself
and others
again

* * *

13

a virtue

a virtue called
acceptance
tells us
once you acknowledge
that something is above
and beneath you
you can
also recognize
the possibility
that you might be
able to
get through it too

what could be the outcome
from when we deny
what is going on
what comes after when
we ignore or pretend
that such an occurrence
was not happening
in any way

we could slow up and
slow down
and delay
our healing

but when we face
and accept reality
we move fast
and we progress
towards recovery

* * *

14

～

reserved

in life
there is always something
you would want
the most
to achieve

but, in case you do not get it
do not fret
instead, find some goodness
in that experience

in the end
you would thank
your stars
for it

as they are
slowly
leading
you towards
the stage of winning

as your fate
would have it
just believe
there is
something
that is best
and that is only reserved
for your unique self

* * *

15

~

a note to my future self

my dear future self
i see that
you are doing
just fine

perhaps, you are even
on your way
to achieving more
meaningful stuff

i could see
you have
greater
things in line

but here's a reminder
for you
as you were
once in my shadow

in a very dark place, you have been
you don't want
to be in
that same
position again

but then
at some point
that could happen
as trials
are inevitable

in such a case
be prepared
remember always
you will find a way
to get through your struggle

* * *

16

new breed

it takes a matter
of humility
to build a tribe
of achievers

show others
they could be better
your goodness
you can share

and together
you can make
a world
of doers

with a common goal
you can shape
and mold
a new breed of go-getters

* * *

17

spectator

in living and loving
come
the art of learning
like the pages of the book that
we read
from page one to the last
we must
be ready to grasp

in watching a movie or a play
some life lessons may
be conveyed
seeing the act one to the last
seeing the entirety
or part of it and
its heart

we may not like
how the story begins and ends
but somehow deep within
there is something to it
there is a part
in it, that touches our heart

in the art of learning
some may choose to participate
some may choose to skip
others may choose to find
other paths
one, or two, could lead
back to it

what happens if we just
browse
as we are not ready
to recognize
the essence in each part
would it still be worth it
to give it a go and try

we could observe how things unravel
we could take part in it in a much ideal way
it is a choice that one has to make
however you decide, you can
learn from it

there is something about
taking on a journey
from some simple ones to the most
daring escapades
that could get us dazzled
the thrill from riding
a roller coaster
to enjoying
a walk on the trail
or the lake, and seeing stunning waterfalls
one can be enthralled
by their charm and
wonder

sometimes the totality
or part in the experience
may seem easy
however, most often
than not
it is not

yet with the choice
that you have to make
you will have to
go through it
anyhow

as for you and me, we may
just be observing
but, somehow
we are
getting it
it may be abstract
as we are looking at
the scope
from many angles

somehow, we could sense
the meaning to it
the whole of it
or just part of it
it doesn't matter
as long as with it, we could relate
and even better
we could feel the moment

* * *

18

gift

if you are asked
what in life is your greatest
achievement
what would first come
to your mind

would that mean wearing
a crown
or belt
the highest prize in a competition
that one
could ever get

would that mean
having accumulated wealth
would that mean
having good health

and --
one could answer, any of these
or even
just one of these

of course, there are more
occurrences in life
that one could think of
from having been born or having been part
of a family that brings you up
or that you are bringing up

and these
what might make us
indeed proud
of all

the truth about
achievement is that
we are all gifted
with something or many things
whatever you may want
to call it
just the same, it is a gift

one, two, three, four
and you can count more
it does not matter
what they are
or how many they are

what matters is
knowing what
we do with these gifts
that
we receive
and continue to receive

* * *

19

commit to achieve

by virtue of doing and
achieving something
we take part in
the process of creating
and co-creating

we are shaping our lives
and take part in the lives of others
in effect, we are bound to
do the act of sharing

in one way or another
we are given talents
from the time
we understand
what could make our life
moving
glowing, growing and
beyond

knowing what we do
with the life that was
bestowed upon us
knowing how we could
make ourselves grow
knowing how we could
help take part in the world

and it would all
start from our little world
our little home
our little steps
that is what achievement could be all
about

achievement and anything
that goes with it takes
some kind of
a commitment to
ourselves
to others
to the world
and most of all to
our ultimate
Creator

* * *

20

doable

aren't we all
responsible
for how the
world goes
in the midst
of the global
crisis
can we not make a
difference

in our little ways
we can initiate steps
in our little ways
we can recover

let us help in caring for our world
let us make our world heavenly and pure
let us make the world worth liveable
let us do our part
it is doable

* * *

21

~

the ride

there was a woman
i met on the train
she asked me where i am going
i said i am on my way
to the last station

i got curious and asked her back
she said she was
on track
she will get off the next
stop

and then, she said
"enjoy the ride
don't be anxious
don't worry
too much
tomorrow is
another day
you'll be
all right."

i was puzzled and
i was not sure
why
she had to say
such an opinion
for which i did not ask

she talks as if she knows me, but
there was no reason
for me to even
mingle
with the woman

i thought
to myself
nothing seems wrong
the train is moving after all
toward
its intended direction

then, i realized
she must have seen
earlier my worrying
frowning face

i was
catching up
on my way
through the entrance
of the train

i worry, though, that
i might be
several minutes
behind

i got up late
on that day
i thought
i would not
make it on the dot
and worse
i would not
be able to meet
my work week's
target

thirty minutes after
i made it on time
no hassle
whatsoever
i got there
as usual

what lesson
might one
learn
from that experience

i contemplate
in here, i
said
to myself

each day, we tend
to focus
on things
that could cause us
to agonize
on some matters
that could
even
push, if not, trigger us

when we could take an
approach
that could give us light
and even
some space to breathe

what is
the point for us
to think
of worries

why not direct
our sight
onto the present
stay calm and radiant

why not
observe
the moment
the surrounding, that
could let us
enjoy the ride

each second of time
so precious
and even though it moves
so fast
in the end
you will find
you are doing
fine

* * *

22

~

keys

a boss once handed a key
to a new employee and said
"tomorrow, you will open the office,
keep up with the cleanliness,
we might have a guest."

the new employee did exactly
what was asked

a week after
the boss asked another
new hiree
to do the same
this time though
no guest is coming

the new hiree
did the instruction
maintained
the office
and even
did some decoration

the boss was happy
with the new employee
as well as the other new hiree

but the boss
was more impressed
and even surprised
by the decoration
the new hiree presented

here, the takeaway was clear
you can be obedient
but you can also take
an extra step
with your
unique strength

you can
go an extra mile
when you use your
creativity
and do it
with
a smile

* * *

23

package

if you are to send
a package
to yourself
what would it be

and--
at such a point
you may contemplate a bit
pause for a while, if need be

give an answer
or make a conclusion
that is not
something
you would like to do
or that would please you

perhaps, that is true
but
did it ever occur to you
to think of
an instance
this way, perhaps
some time ago

of course
such a question
might not make sense
one could wonder
who would do
such a thing

but
if you are to look at it
in a different view
you will find that
the act of sending and receiving
is part
of how humans
communicate
in the outside
and even
in our internal being

do we not examine
how we are feeling
or seeing
things

we may use such a case
as a metaphor
but in truth, if you are
to talk to yourself
what would you say
and how would you say it

we all long for
nurturing, loving messages
we look and wait for
others to give us some
kind of security and love
and to make us
feel great

would you not want
to nourish your
very heart and mind
with self-awareness, care and
tenderness
as though they are all wrapped
in a package
for you to unbox
and it will fill you up however you want

then it would
remind you again
such nourishment can
all start from yourself, from within

know every part
of yourself
bit by bit
know what your life
truly means

in case of crisis
know what will
make you persist
and dwell

in the end
you will find meaning
in every course of action
that you take
and it can allow you
to grow
from within, from every little success
that you make

* * *

24

~

perspective

when you capture
the moment

when you give life to
a dime a dozen scene

when you put
a whole new meaning
to a tiresome day

when you declare
to yourself
you want
to overcome
a long, tedious day

when you would
like to explore
a whole new adventure

when you are engrossed
to find
a precious gem

when you would like
to hike
to reach the peak of the mountain

when you
spend
a rare moment

when you give
life
to a whole new dimension

when you see
life in
a new horizon

you can then
realize for yourself how breathtaking
every scene
can be

every moment
can
be
marvelous and exciting

you can then realize
there is more
to what you
experience

you just have to go out there
witness
how each step
leads you
to a world of amazement

you can then put your
life into
a whole new perspective

and it can all begin
with one thing

take one step closer to
the remarkable moment
and all it takes is to
believe

* * *

25

big

someone prefers
to be mediocre
to remain in a status quo

someone else wondered
why not change
direction
what's wrong
with thinking big
is it the mere thought of it
is it about the details
that go with bigness
is it the lack of confidence
that could stop
one to be a dreamer
to pursue
thinking bigger

whatever it may be
that can stop
one to think big
why not
do it anyway

dream big
o, such a moment
it is free to do that
feel it, be in it

dream big
o, such a moment
it is when you can direct
your little steps
to where it should go

dream big
o, such a moment
it is when you can start
from being small

dream big
o, such a moment
it is by doing so
that you can set your goal

* * *

26

in choosing one thing

you can choose one thing
that interest
you the most
it does not matter what it is
as long as
you are inclined
to do it

and you do not just
simply do it
for the sake of
getting done with it

but you do it with
your highest
intent
with what you possess
with your improved skills and
with your unique strength

should you become a mess
with your process
you can always reassess
until
you could be at your best

you would still perform better
this way
perhaps, a lot better than others
and even your contemporary

* * *

27

up there

you may be afraid to move up
because you are not
familiar with the new setup
you have not
been there
and things may not look easy
up, above

but take heart
know that
others might have been there too
even much earlier
perhaps, many more years
before you

and if you would ask them
whether they made it through
or not
you would learn that
it only takes enough courage
to make it
on your way to the top

and if you give up
at any point
you will not ever see
what is it like
being up there
and that could forfeit
the reality for which
you intended

* * *

28

match

nothing in what we did
was set in bricks
someone asked
should there be
some match
or some tricks

if there was
how could we find
who knows
you might exhibit some kicks
you might use some arrows
you might miss some turns
you might see some cracks
how could we define
what that means

you bet
it could get
through your bones
and you alone
could know what else
must you do
to get cracking
to finding
the key or code

then, all of a sudden
a rare call
signals
and then it rings
in an unexpected moment
it stops for a second
and then it rings again
this time it would not stop
until somebody picks it up

and whatever place
you might be in
must you stop with what
you are doing
who knows what
sort of surprise
might that bring

* * *

29

at stake

do you ever attempt
to try to change
someone
or do you attempt
to change
yourself

which one
do you find harder
to try

or--
which one seems
way
impossible

when you attempt
to change
others
you are setting yourself up
to something
fragile and brittle

you must know that
you could be doing something
that might equate to risks
and the stakes are high

for one
you can never be in control
of another person's
mind
and soul

when you attempt to change
yourself
you are setting yourself up
to become
the improver of
your
very own mind and soul

* * *

30

container

we seek for what
could fill a space

we seek for what
could fill up
empty bottles

then we see half-filled
container

we do not stop from there
we still
need to fill
the gap

then we see holes
the container
needs
some kind of
repair

get the container fixed
find some material
to patch up
the set of holes in it

there are
two choices
available

fix it for
whatever
it can do for
now

or--
fix it for good even
if it means
you will
wait a while

* * *

31

~~

project

do not get caught up
with the task
at hand
you can immerse
with it
but always, always
learn to rise

there are more tasks
to be accomplished
even more complex ones
treat each task as
a golden step
that can lead towards
the next

you could learn fast
or you could try to master
but be forewarned
not all tasks
have the same weight
but regardless of its
nature
the objective in it
you can capture

* * *

32

ironic

how ironic it is to say
you try to do your best
but hardly anyone could see
the greatness in it

you try to do the opposite
almost immediately
others could see it
and even criticize
you for it

it is human nature, so to say
even we can sing
some kind of a hymn
or jingle
in the end
we turn
to the old habit

do good and even be better
others will forget
do things that may be bad
you can bet
no one can forget

and then
that will make you sad

then we repeat
to try to do better
you bet
others will forget

do the worst
in the planet
you'll be sad
no one would forget

* * *

33

prudent

if you are intelligent
almost automatically
others might expect
you are someone prudent

and you would be careful
with what you say
with what you do
with what you create

be forewarned
being intelligent may be a rare
breed

for even if every man was gifted
with intellect and free will
others may have opted
not to use it
the same way you did

others can brand you as
an elitist, or above a mediocre
or a person of high calibre, perhaps

you may not belong to
the same league of artists
still, you may appear of different class
with which
others cannot relate

yet time will come
many people
would look up to you
for your words, your policies
even your rare invention

and once they are
introduced
and get accustomed to your
creation
they subscribe to it
they use it
they make it viral and
even talk about it
with others

in the end
others will see and approve
your rare creation
and that it can help improve
their way of living

and it all
starts with
one intelligent being
whom people all
brand
as prudent

* * *

34

feeding

like a plant that
needs tending
a pet that
needs caring
a house that
needs cleaning
a yard that
needs sweeping
a floor that needs
mopping

we need to clear out
negativity from our mind
we need to mop out
ambiguous, clouded thoughts

we need to feed
our mind
with positive affirmation
with loving thoughts
with conviction
with our life's governing principles
by which we believe
and keep us able and willing
to listen

we need gentleness
to allow
goodness to enter
our heart and soul

* * *

About the Author

Sheila Atienza is a Canadian book author, digital media artist, and marketing professional based in B.C., Canada. She is also an award-winning filmmaker, actress, and passionate content creator.

Sheila explores nonfiction, fiction, and poetry. Some of her published works/books are available in:

University of Toronto Thomas Fisher Library; McGill University; Dalhousie University DAL Killam Library; Brown University; Library and Archives nationales du Québec; Canada Mortgage Housing Corporation; Medicine Hat College; Loyalist College; and other libraries across Canada and the U.S.A.

Sheila is the author of the books: "Beauty in Love and Sorrows," "A Wacky, Rocky World: Just a Teeny Little Voice," "Tweets for Your Thoughts," and many other publications.

Sheila's books are available through bookstores and online retailers worldwide.